THE
POWER
OF
PIE

HOW A MAN OF COLOR AND
FOLLOWER OF CHRIST
SUCCEEDED IN CORPORATE AMERICA

RUSSELL GROSS

urbanpress

Urban Press
P.O. Box 8881
Pittsburgh, PA 15221-0881
412.646.2780
www.urbanpress.us

TABLE OF CONTENTS

Dedication   **V**
Introduction   **VII**

The Journey   **1**
Mentors and Coaches   **7**
The Value of Networking   **17**
The Power of PIE   **25**
The Power of I and E   **31**
E for Exposure   **43**
The Intersection of P I and E   **53**

Epilogue   **59**
Author's Note   **61**

TABLE OF CONTENTS

Dedication

Introduction

The Journey

Mentors and Coaches

The Value of Networking

Power of III

The Power of I and II

The Power

III. Intersection of II and III

Notes

DEDICATION

I want to dedicate this book to all the coaches and mentors who helped me become the person I am, so that I could enjoy career success and also become the man of God He envisioned I could be. None of us can make it by ourselves. Everybody needs somebody in some way every day, and I am no exception. Therefore, I salute and thank all the men and women who thought I was worth helping. I couldn't have had the life I've had or the life I am having in this season of my life without you. I truly believe my best days are yet to come!

I've had many excellent coaches and mentors speak into my life, and they are too numerous to mention. I do want to specifically acknowledge and thank Harvey Coleman, founder and CEO of Coleman Consulting in Atlanta, Georgia, and the father of the PIE principle, which is the subject of this book. I met Mr. Coleman only one time back in the late '70s or early '80s when he came to teach a course at the New England Telephone Company (now part of Verizon), but that encounter changed my career and life. That course focused on three keys to career success, which he referred to as the principles of PIE. From then until my retirement from the corporate world in 2016, the principles of PIE played a major role in the career success I achieved, as well as in my personal life. So thank you, Mr. Coleman. You probably never knew how much you impacted my life, but you certainly did in ways I never could have imaged.

INTRODUCTION

This book is intended for anyone and everyone who works for a living. While written by an African-American follower of Jesus Christ who had two successful corporate careers, this book is for people just coming into the workplace who want to know how to succeed in the corporate world; people who have been in the workplace for a while but may not be where they thought they would be at this point in their career and want to do something about it; and for people who have left the workplace, perhaps in retirement as I am, and who want to succeed in their post-corporate phase of life. The principles in this book can also be applied in anyone's personal and public life outside of the workplace. As I said, this book is for anyone and everyone regardless of race, ethnicity, gender, age, or faith.

As I started work on this book, I was looking out at the ocean view from the window of my vacation condo on a crisp early-May morning, thinking back to June 21, 1970. That's when it all began, the first day of my journey as a black man through corporate America. I had just graduated from college a week earlier with a degree in civil engineering and was reporting for my first day of work. Little did I know that this journey would not end until 46 years later, after two successful careers, several home relocations, and many lessons learned.

When I retired in 2016 and transitioned into my next phase of life, writing a book about this journey was the farthest thing from my mind, even though I had already published one book and would have a second one published shortly thereafter. After considering the advice of many people, I began to think I did have something to share that may be helpful to other black men who were starting or in the midst of their own journey through corporate America. In fact, I concluded it would be helpful to *any* person of color (man or woman) or of any ethnicity for that matter, and especially for followers of Christ, who were on a similar journey.

While never a corporate CEO or senior executive, I held many middle and upper management positions, and for the last ten years of my career held an executive position. While I had a successful career, it could have been better if I had chosen to make different decisions at critical points in my corporate experience. God was leading me, however, and I chose to follow His will, die to self, and submit to His plan. For that, I have no regrets and would not change a single thing about the path I took on my journey as it all helped shape and mold me into who I am today.

In this book, I am writing about the power of PIE from the perspective of a man who applied these principles throughout his career with positive results. I will share what worked, what didn't work, and what might have worked during my career, in the hope that they will help you in your journey through the corporate world.

If you think that simply working hard and keeping your nose clean will get you ahead and move you up the corporate ladder, think again! My career may have started way back in 1970, and a lot has changed since then, but what I will share in this book is still applicable in the corporate environment I left not too long ago. As an added benefit, many of the concepts and principles I discuss in this book can be used in your personal life's journey as well.

Let me whet your appetite by telling you a bit about the PIE principles that are the focus of this book. PIE stands for performance, image, and exposure, three keys to succeeding in the corporate world. People spend most of their work lives striving to become excellent performers at whatever their job and career entail. Being an excellent performer is necessary to get you into the "game," so to speak, but really counts for about 10% of succeeding in corporate America. Performance is your admission ticket to potential career success. Once that is in place, image and exposure contribute the other 90% to get ahead. Projecting the "right" image gets you in front of the "right" people who can impact your career. That may seem simple and you may you think you know all you need to know about PIE, but I urge you to be patient and read on. This book isn't that long and will pay immediate as well as long-term dividends!

I pray you enjoy reading this and are blessed in whatever your professional and life journeys may be. Once you finish, share this book with others who may be able to benefit from the *Power of PIE*. As you do, share a story or two of how PIE have already impacted your life and career.

Russell Gross
Attleboro, Massachusetts
May 2018

THE JOURNEY

Let me share more of my corporate journey with you before we proceed. I spent more than 25 years in the telecommunications industry in the old Bell Telephone System, a little more than nineteen years in healthcare, with about nine months between the two in a fundraising position with the United Way. My first position was part of a special program that hired students out of college. That program would years later be the subject of a class action lawsuit due to the low pay level for those hired compared to others in similar positions.

In this program, we were placed in a second-level management position and given one year to demonstrate the potential to be able to perform at the next level and higher in the next three to five years. If we didn't show that potential, we were terminated after the first year. Ironically, they didn't tell us those things until after we started. Remember, it was 1970 so employers could get away with that kind of practice.

In my case, I took the job since I was offered an increase before I even accepted the position and had no knowledge at that time of periodic position salary adjustment increases. I also took the job because it was in the next town over from where I grew up in Rhode Island, so I could still live at home with my parents until I got myself somewhat established. I was one of a small number of people of color nationwide who were hired into the program and was informed I was the first person put into a construction manager position. You also should know that only about one out of three people hired into this program succeeded.

I was managing and working with primarily older white men, some of whom were my parents' age or older, some who knew my parents and had known me since I was a child, and who resented working for a twenty-one-year-old "N____" (you can fill in the blanks) just out of college. My boss was a 60-year-old alcoholic who wanted to prove one of these college hires could survive in the construction environment and he also wanted to show off his person of color. I can't tell you how difficult that year was, but by the grace and mercy of God and with help from supportive parents, I made it!

After that first year, I worked as an engineering manager in the same office for two years when I met my first mentor and coach (more on that in future chapters). Then I was transferred to the regional corporate office in Boston where I worked in the revenue matters department. There I met two more mentors and coaches. I was responsible for development of residential and business customer telephone rates and supporting the defense of those rates before state regulatory commissions.

After three years, I transferred to systems development where I worked on a team responsible for project management of a New England implementation of an automated accounting system being installed across the entire Bell System. It was on this assignment that I met one of the most significant mentors and coaches in my life who trained and coached me, opening doors for me instead of furthering his own career. That led to my being considered the best project manager in the Bell System and a promotion in 1979 to district manager at AT&T as nationwide project manager for the automated accounting system I had managed in New England.

Within a period of six months, I had a new job in New York City, a new wife, a new son, and a new home in central New Jersey. That represented a whole lot of change for a young man who up to that point had lived and worked in New England his entire life. During my four years on this job I learned what commuting was all about, enjoyed the sights and sounds of New York City (including the infamous Studio 54), and began to learn how to be a husband and father. It was also during this time in June 1980 that I gave my life to the Lord, the best decision I ever made and *the* decision that changed my life forever!

In 1983, I was called back to Boston and the local Bell System company in New England to take over project management of the local implementation of the Bell System facility assignment system that had not been going well. The executive I was under when I managed the implementation of the accounting system several years earlier remembered what I had done and wanted me back to fix the problems with implementing the facility assignment system, which fortunately I was able to. With this return to New England, my wife, son, and I bought and moved into the house I still live in today. After three years, I transferred to the corporate planning department where I was trained as a professional regulatory witness responsible for defending the costs charged to the local company in New England by NYNEX, the new parent company of the old New England Telephone and New York Telephone companies after the breakup of the Bell System. I still sought out and had the benefit of coaches and mentors, but also realized that I was becoming a coach and mentor myself to more and more people.

The expression that what goes around comes around manifested itself in my life in 1991 when I was sought after to go back to the place where I started in 1970, but this time as the director of the entire department, now called engineering and construction. The general manager who sought me out and who would become a friend, coach, and mentor of mine, did so because he was impressed with how I led the Minority Management Association. MMA was an employee-based and founded organization started in 1979 to support development, training, and advancement of minority employees in the company.

Having been a charter member, I served as vice president and then president of the organization in the late eighties and early nineties. My last position in telecommunications came in 1993 when I became director of business planning (same as strategic planning) for Massachusetts and Rhode Island. In December of 1995, I took advantage of a great opportunity and took early retirement. Too young to really retire, I decided to pursue a second career.

After a brief stint with the United Way, in 1997 I

accepted the position of senior planner with an integrated health system in Rhode Island and quickly learned that skills are transferrable from industry to industry. Realizing the importance of mentors and having been a mentor myself, I became part of the company's initial mentoring program and was handpicked by the CEO to be part of his mentoring group due in part to his friendship from his days in New York with an executive I knew from my telecommunication days who was then the CEO of Verizon. After a couple of years, I was promoted to planning manager and in December 2006 was promoted to an executive position as senior director of strategic planning, a position I held until retiring in October 2016 and transitioning to the next assignment the Lord had for my life, which I am living out now.

Those are the work details of my journey, and the rest of this book will attempt to share the lessons and principles I learned that helped me to be successful as a black man in corporate America, with a focus on the power of PIE.

MENTORS AND COACHES

In the previous chapter describing my journey through corporate America, I made several references to mentors and coaches. Now I want to share my thoughts with you on the importance of mentors and coaches; how you find them; how you become one and why that's important; and the role mentors and coaches played in my corporate journey. Later, I'll talk about how mentors and coaches fit in with each component of PIE.

The Definition

Let's start by defining our concepts. In short and in broad terms, mentors help you move ahead to the next and future levels in your life and vocation, while coaches help you excel at what you are doing now in your life and vocation.

Mentors and coaches are not just people who help you in your vocation, job, or career, but also in your life journey as well. Mentors are people who have achieved things in their lives and vocations that you have not, which may or may not be exactly what you want to achieve.

Through those successes, they have gained insight, knowledge, and experience in realizing their dreams and goals that can help you achieve yours. Mentors are wise and trusted counselors and teachers, as well as more senior (usually but not always in level and age) influencers, sponsors, and supporters. They are people who have taken an interest in you and your future, have your best interests at heart, expect you to follow their guidance, and will not generally give you any further guidance until you do the last thing they told you to do.

On the other hand, coaches are people who instruct, train, teach, and tutor you to excel at what you are currently doing in your position in or outside of the workplace, such as your present job, something you are doing in your community or church, or in your family situation. Coaches may not always have your best interests at heart, especially in the workplace, since they are often directed by their bosses to help you, and their motivation can be based on what's in it for them (or the company) instead of trying to help you be the best you can be. Therefore, it's a good practice to seek out your own coaches in addition to those who may be assigned to you. Also note that coaches help you excel to be the very best you can be at what you currently do, but not to be perfect, since no one is or ever can be perfect.

Mentors and coaches can be the same person, but more often than not are different people. The people who can help you move ahead may not be able to coach you because of where they are right now, or because their functional expertise is not in the same area as your current position. Similarly, the people who can help you excel are often not able to help you move forward to your desired future work or life because they haven't achieved the kind of success that has given them the insight, knowledge, or experience to help you move toward your dreams and goals, or their current position doesn't equip them to help you in that way.

Their Importance

So why are mentors and coaches important? The short answer is that the Lord told us they are. We know from the Word that God's intention is for all in the body of Christ to help each other in their walk as they further God's kingdom on the earth (see Ephesians 4:11-16). In fact, Jesus told us that when He returned to the Father, He would send another to be with and in us; to walk beside us to help us remember what Jesus said and how to apply that Word in our daily lives; to teach and instruct us; to comfort, help, pray for us, and so on. This One sent to help is the Holy Spirit, the supreme mentor and coach, if you will (see John 14:15-18).

We also realize that God speaks to, helps, and guides us through other people as well as through His Holy Spirit (parents, spouses, spiritual leaders, other believers, etc.). Therefore, God expects us to help each other serving as mentors and coaches where appropriate.

Even in the natural, none of us is foolish enough to really think we know it all about any one thing, let alone everything. Why should we try to learn and do every-thing on our own when there are people out there who already know how to do what we are trying to do, and know it better than we do? They know how to help us achieve our dreams and goals because they have already achieved theirs. It doesn't make much sense to try and invent the way when others have already traveled it.

I hope you can see that from both a spiritual and natural perspective, it makes sense that we need both coaches and mentors in our lives. They can open doors for us that we cannot, they see things we can't see because they've already been there, and they teach and instruct us in the finer points of what we are trying to do, just to name a few of the benefits of having them in our lives. I am sure there are more, but these are the reasons from my perspective as to the importance of and why we need mentors and coaches.

Finding a Coach

How then do we find the mentors and coaches we need at any given time? We seek them out, asking God's wisdom in the search. Whenever I needed or still need help in my life from a mentor, coach, or any other type of individual, I always start by seeking God's wisdom on the matter according to James 1:5-8 and then following His lead. That said, sometimes coaches come to you, especially in the workplace where you are new on the job and a co-worker is assigned to teach and train you. Those may not always be the best coaches, so I suggest you seek your own coaches, be it inside or outside the workplace.

How do you do that? Look for people who are already performing with excellence at what you do right now or are getting ready to do in the near future. Remember, coaches help you improve your performance in your present position or situation. In the workplace, they may be coworkers or people in your company who previously had your job but transferred or moved on to another department or company. A coach outside of the workplace may take a little more effort to locate, but they are there. You may have to ask other people for leads and referrals in and outside your company to find people who excel at what you do. With all the technology available to us today, along with the Internet and social media, there really aren't any excuses for not finding good coaches.

When you do identify someone who would be a good person from whom you can learn, seek them out, letting them know you are impressed by what they do or a particular skill they have and ask them if they are willing to coach or teach you how to do what they do so you can excel at it as they have. Most people are flattered that you ask and are willing to help you. Then be flexible and willing to work with them around their availability, not yours. You should show your appreciation by asking what you can do to help them, and being ready to help if they give you something that you are able to do.

If people you seek out can't or don't want to help, or more commonly don't have the time even after you are willing to adjust your schedule to fit theirs, thank them for their time and consideration and seek out the next possible coach you identified during your initial search. It is always a good idea to identify more than one potential coach (or mentor) during your initial search, because at different times in a career or life journey, you will need coaches and mentors with varying skills and experiences.

Finding a Mentor

Seeking a mentor is like seeking a coach, but there are some differences as you look for someone to guide you toward realizing your career aspirations or life goals. Sometimes mentors will seek you out when they see something in you that they had when they were at the stage of your career or life journey. Express your gratitude for them taking an interest in you, and agree to at least an initial meeting to identify how he or she might be able to help you. At the same time, do your homework before you meet to see what that person has achieved and how that person has lived. Do they have anything you can learn from them to help you in your quest?

Even if there doesn't appear to be anything, take the first meeting because you never know. I never said no to anyone who wanted to mentor me because even though they may not have what I needed right then, somewhere down the road that person may have been able to help me or open a door for me. In addition, both you and the potential mentor should be able to tell when you meet if either it's not a good match or the chemistry is not right for you to be able to effectively work together.

Most of the time, you need to seek out your mentors, and for the most part they are going to be people with whom you do not have immediate or direct access. Start the process the same way you do with coaches. Identify those who may be able to help you achieve your dreams and long-term goals by discovering what they did to get where they are that can help you get where you want to go. This will take more than a minute to do and needs to have your full attention. Also, as with coaches, identify multiple possible mentors because as you make progress on your career and life journey, you will need multiple mentors along the way.

Once you have identified potential mentors, the real work starts as you work to gain access to them. From a business career perspective, your potential mentors may not even know who you are or that you exist. If they do, it's often that they heard someone mention your name but don't really know much about you. Sometimes your potential mentors are in the same company or department as you, but several levels removed from you.

Even if a potential mentor does know who you are and may not be that much removed from you, the issue isn't just them knowing who you are, but gaining access to them and their time, getting on their calendar to have an audience with them. Remember, mentors are people who can guide you in what you need to do to get to where you aspire to be, and in some cases are in a decision-making position where they can have a direct impact on your career. So how do you gain access to potential mentors?

You access them by any means possible! Do whatever it takes to get fifteen to thirty minutes with them to start. It could be as simple as calling their office to get on their calendar, but usually it takes more than that. Often you need to work through a series of other people to get to the one who can really help you. In my case, there have been a few times when I started by meeting with people I knew to talk about my career aspirations, making it clear the type of people I am trying to get in front of. I even dropped a few names in hopes the person I was meeting with might have a connection with one of those people, connect me with someone else who did, or give me referrals to other people I had not identified who might be potential mentors.

I've found that it was usually the third or fourth meeting where I connected with the right person, but almost every time I picked up a few things that were helpful from the people in the earlier meetings. Another way to access mentors is to try and schedule informational interviews, which you usually conduct not in hopes of landing a job or new position, but just to become known to an influential person or organization that might be helpful in the future. This is how I eventually moved into healthcare from telecommunications. The informational interview meetings can also be used, however, to connect with or gain a referral that could eventually connect you with a potential mentor.

Another way to connect with potential mentors is to find out where they might be speaking, attending an event, playing golf or tennis, or staying while traveling. If you have that information, do all you can to meet them. That's not the time to try and start the mentoring relationship, but a time to meet and make a connection so that when you try to schedule a meeting with them later, there is a chance they will remember you and agree to the meeting.

Those random meetings are usually quick and don't give you much time with the potential mentor, so you need to be prepared with a brief ten to fifteen second introductory statement that states who you are, what you do, the service you provide, and why it's an honor to meet them. This is all part of the art of networking, which I'll cover in the next chapter. This practice is not only helpful as you try to meet potential mentors, but also as you attempt to make helpful business connections that expand both your professional and personal networks.

A similar way to connect with potential mentors as well as make good business connections is getting in front of them so they can see and hear you. Most people form opinions about other people based upon what they see, hear, and read about that person. For example, I volunteered to run the United Way campaign at my company since I knew people who impacted my career would be there and see and hear me at the kick-off meetings at various company locations. This method led to many important business connections as well as future meetings with potential mentors. Attending and participating in company outings such as charity golf tournaments and charity races and walks can accomplish the same thing but in a more social and relaxed setting. Finally, sometimes you can connect with potential mentors just by chance.

The last thing I want to mention about connecting with mentors is that you need to do your homework and be prepared when you do finally meet with a potential mentor. You probably won't have much time so know what you want to ask and talk about, and have a way to end the meeting with the stage set for the next meeting. As my pastor says, have your two questions ready for the fifteen minutes you'll probably have with that potential mentor or business connection. Also, ask for wisdom about the "how" of what the person did to get where they are instead of what they did to get where they are, and you may very well get more time, more questions, and more insight to help you on your journey.

The Relationship with a Mentor

Mentor and mentee relationships are just that – a relationship and not a friendship. I have had long-lasting relationships with my most effective mentors that have carried over into my retirement. Mentor and mentee relationships are also not just one way. Mentors can learn a few things from their mentees, including things about themselves. In addition, seeking mentors is not just about getting something but also about giving something. The mentee may possibly be able to do something for the mentor, or the mentee may become a mentor as he or she moves along in the journey to realize his or her aspirations.

If we are only about getting, never having an attitude of gratitude to help somebody else out and sharing what we learned along our own journey that would be a blessing to others, then God is not going to bless us and open doors we can't open for ourselves. Someone took the time to give you life-impacting wisdom, so consequently you need to be willing to do the same! Look for opportunities to mentor others and offer to do so, or be receptive when people seek you out as a mentor.

I can't begin to tell you how important having mentors and coaches has been in both my professional and personal life. They taught me, trained me, helped me to perform with excellence, guided me, shared their wisdom and insights with me, opened doors for me, supported and encouraged me, corrected me, and cut me off when I did not do the last thing they asked me to do. While everyone needs coaches and mentors, they are essential for people of color and in particular black males trying to realize their dreams and goals in a world still dominated by white males.

All the progress I made and success I had during my journey through corporate America involved multiple coaches and mentors along the way. Never underestimate the value of coaches and mentors to your journey. Seek them out and humble yourself by submitting to their expertise and wisdom. For their help, have an attitude of gratitude and then seek to serve the same role in the lives of others. Now let's turn our attention to the practice of networking, which I mentioned earlier.

THE VALUE OF NETWORKING

If you are going to succeed at anything in life, whether professional or personal, it is going to require some degree of networking. Finding and working effectively with coaches and mentors will involve some networking skills. Making helpful business contacts and hooking up with people who can open doors or facilitate access to people or financial resources for you require networking. Networking helps you to make friends, become more social, and become known.

To succeed in the business world or corporate America, understanding and applying the finer points of networking is critical, and they include what you say, how and when you say it, how you dress, your body language, how you approach people in specific situations, and much more. Sharing all the details of various networking techniques is not the focus of this book, but it is important to have some understanding of what networking is and the basics of how to network. I found this tool to be important to success in corporate America, especially for people of color and specifically black men. More on that later.

I have seen various definitions of networking, but there are two that I like. One is a noun that describes what networking is and the other is a verb that describes how networking functions. The noun defines networking as *forming associations of individuals having common interests to provide mutual assistance, information, help, and the like*. Note that the association is mutual, in that each member of the association is expected to give as well as receive so that all in the association benefit. That resembles what I mentioned in the previous chapter on coaches and mentors. It's a two-way street on which each helps and provides value for the other.

It is also related to how God expects His children to work together for the benefit of the entire Body, rather than for individual benefit or gain. If we think about it, we all have associations or networks we rely on to succeed in the workplace, in our families, with friends, in our churches, and in various other public and community-based settings. We may not always call these associations networks, but that is what they are. Sometimes we call them cliques, peer groups, our homies, a support group, and so on.

We all have them, and if you take a minute to think about how you got into and used them, you will have a good idea of how networking functions. The problem is that we are comfortable networking with people we know or who are like us in terms of race, gender, or age, but not so comfortable when we step out of our comfort zone and network with people who are different than we are or with whom we have little in common. Unfortunately, to make the contacts we need, as well as to find coaches and mentors to help us move forward and grow, we must step out of our comfort zones to engage people who are not like us.

This leads to the verb definition of networking, which speaks more to how networking works. It defines networking as *cultivating people who can be helpful professionally or personally, especially in finding employment, moving to a higher position, or bettering oneself socially, economically, spiritually, or physically*. Just as understanding what the concept of *mutual* means and how it applies to the noun definition of networking, we must understand what *cultivate* means and how it applies to the verb definition of networking.

There are numerous definitions for the verb *cultivate*, but from a practical standpoint, I define it as *being able to develop, nurture, and evolve something*. Further, to nurture something is to rear, bring up, and mold in order to grow it, while the concept of evolving something means to move toward it gradually. Therefore, networking is about developing and molding relationships over time with people who can be helpful to you professionally and personally. Obviously, this requires finding effective people and developing interpersonal skills, which we all have and with dedication and effort, we can all develop even more fully.

As I said with mentors and coaches, this book is not intended to lay out all the details of effective networking, but to move you to consider a few things. There are other factors you may want to include in your networking strategy depending on your purpose for networking and what you are trying to accomplish. These are a few that are essential in my mind.

1. Make networking a regular activity.

This is a good way to get started if you are not used to networking outside your comfort zone. Two or three times a week you should reach out to someone you find interesting. Don't ask for anything, just say hello and let the person know you admire what they do or what they stand for. Show interest in what they do. You can best do this by email, particularly if it's someone within your company or industry. Finding someone's email address should not be too difficult and can usually be obtained with a phone call to their office, searching their or their company's website, or from social media. I would advise against contacting these people via public social media, since most people you really want to network with get many views and likes and don't respond publicly.

2. Don't be an Internet panhandler.

Most people will ask for things online through social media or email they would not ask for in person. In addition, people tend to keep asking for things much of the time, and can become demanding in their requests, rather than simply trying to connect and then later cultivate the relationship. True networking doesn't start with your hand extended for help.

3. Know who you are reaching out to.

This is quite important when trying to connect with influential people, not because of their importance per se but because they have a lot of people reaching out to them. By doing your homework and getting to know facts about the person beyond surface information most people would know, you can stand out. Influential people are often flattered someone knows about some of their work and how it helped them or why it piqued their interest. Find out what issue the person is passionate about and mention it in your email, and your chances of being remembered or getting a response are greatly enhanced.

4. Use positive language.

Employ respectful and considerate language regardless of whether you are communicating via email, text, social media, or in person. For example, if you are trying to get a meeting with someone, say something like "I'd really appreciate it if we could meet sometime for no more than thirty minutes at your convenience to discuss how you went about completing that last project of yours [be specific] as I am working on something similar and could benefit from your wise counsel." What you should not say is something like, "I need to meet with you for about thirty minutes this Thursday to find out how you got that last project (again be specific) done so I can complete one I'm working on the same way."

5. Cultivate your power contacts.

We've already covered what cultivating relationships is about, but the point here is that all your contacts are not equal. You need to determine which contacts are going to be helpful in achieving your goals. Are they people who will teach, train, guide, give you wise counsel, open doors, help you gain access for you to resources you need, or connect you with others who are the people with whom you want to gain an audience. These are contacts where the cultivation has progressed to a point where the give-and-take between you both is at a high level and each of you is willing to help and support the other when possible.

6. Learn how to use email effectively.

Every email or face-to-face communication is not the same. While doing initial outreach, you want to keep your communication simple and short, focusing on the person you are contacting and why you are interested in connecting with them. If you can identify a mutual connection, be it a friend or interest, all the better. With established contacts, the communication changes or shifts, just like it would when talking with someone you have been friends with for a while. Make sure the only time you contact or meet with them is not just when you want something. Connect or meet to get caught up because you enjoy each other's company. Make sure your emails or other communications with established contacts are interesting, with content they will enjoy or insightful questions or thoughts that appeal to both of you.

7. Don't expect anything.

This skill is extremely important if you are going to be a successful networker. When you are always out to get something, you're just trying to manipulate the other person rather than network with them, be it intentional or not. Your mindset should not be expecting to get something right away. Instead, it will benefit you in the long run to build a comprehensive network because when you do, the long-term results will flow more naturally then if you constantly try to pester people for things you want or need. When you network effectively, what you need often comes unsolicited from someone in your network, perhaps even people you least expected. So instead of your focus being on getting, focus on great conversation and information exchange with smart people, introductions to other new people, and simply creating a personality that people enjoy knowing and like.

8. Burn useless bridges.

I wrote earlier that I never turn down a meeting with a potential coach or mentor. This point seems to contradict that. Sooner or later, however, you are going to meet people you should not and don't want to be like, people who just want to drain you of what you can do to help them, without ever offering anything in return. They just keep asking without giving or even trying to cultivate a relationship with you. That's not what networking is about, and you need to cut these people off. You don't have to be rude, but let them know you don't want to be around them as long as they have a vulture-like mentality.

Sometimes you just ignore their calls and emails, and if you come face-to-face with them and they ask why you haven't gotten back to them, just say you've been busy, tied up, or something else along those lines. After a while, they will get the message. There may be times, however, when they don't get the message, and then you need to be honest with them and tell them why you don't want to be around them.

9. Be prepared.

This applies more to face-to-face communication than emails, texts, or social media. Know how to make yourself known in fifteen seconds or less, communicating who you are, your skill or the value you provide to people, and why it's your pleasure to meet the person. If in a first-time meeting, be sure you have the questions ready you want to ask, with your top two right at the top of your list since those may be the only two you get to ask. Also, be sure you have a way to end the meeting that sets the stage for the next or follow up meeting.

As I said earlier, this book is not intended to provide a detailed tutorial on networking, but rather is presented to help you understand the basics of what networking is, how it works, and its value in helping you succeed in achieving your professional and life visions, dreams, and goals. Now let's talk more about the *Power of PIE*.

THE POWER OF PIE

So far, I have shared three key tools I found essential to successfully implement the principles of PIE and experience the full power of those principles in both your professional and personal life. Now, let's go deeper into the *Power of PIE*.

1. The Power of P

Let's start with the P in PIE, which was the first key to my success and will be to yours. P stands for performance, which means to carry out, execute, or do something in the proper, customary, established, or prescribed manner. It is the day-to-day work you are tasked with doing and the results you deliver. In terms of the power of PIE, the goal is to strive for excellent performance, being the very best you can be at whatever you are doing at any given time. Notice that I didn't say *perfect* performance because everyone makes mistakes from time to time. But those mistakes should be the exception rather than the rule, and should become fewer and fewer as you evolve toward becoming an excellent performer – the very best you can be!

To become an excellent performer takes time, hard work, a lot of effort, failure, persistence, and the help of coaches, which we discussed earlier. You won't become an excellent performer overnight. What's more, beauty is in the eye of the beholder, so those who behold your performance must also concur that you are performing at a high level. Everyone likes to think we are great at what we do, but if that is the case, why doesn't everyone get an excellent performance evaluation each year from their supervisor?

In fact, the performance may be exceptional, but sometimes the results are not recognized or appreciated by those around you. That's why it is important to seek out periodic feedback from others as to how you are doing – bosses, customers, and co-workers. One way to do that is to develop a mindset of appreciation and gratitude when people give you feedback on your performance when you ask what you are good at, what you can do better, or where your work is falling short of what others need to perform their jobs. You need to express your appreciation whether you agree with the feedback or not because the perception of others is the reality you must address.

Once again, this is where coaches become important, for they can help you improve your performance in skill or attitudinal areas. For coaches to be beneficial to you, however, you must be teachable and receptive to what they suggest you start, stop, or improve doing. This is the reason it's good to get feedback from a variety of people in order to validate your strengths, weaknesses, and areas in need of improvement. Don't be offended or take the feedback personally, but receive it as constructive criticism, and then find a coach or coaches who can help you improve that area of your performance.

It also takes failure to become an excellent performer. What do I mean by that? If you go back to the basic definition of performance, it speaks to doing things in a customary, prescribed, or established manner. If you are doing things well in the customary, prescribed, or established manner, then you are a good and maybe even a great performer, but not an excellent performer. You must be a good or great performer before you can be an *excellent* performer, which requires that you fail along the way. Failure on the way to becoming a good or great performer requires performing in the customary, prescribed, and established manner until you get it right. Then you work to excel at performing in the customary, prescribed, or established manner.

To fail on the way to becoming an excellent performer involves trying something new and different after you've become a good or great performer. That allows you to perform more effectively and efficiently, and with a higher quality result than when you performed in the customary, prescribed, or established manner. I can almost guarantee that the first time you try something new or different, you will either fail or won't get the improved results, quality, efficiency, or effectiveness you were aiming at. When that occurs, don't give up or get frustrated. Rather, try something else new or a different approach to the new thing that didn't quite work the first time.

You see, if you don't try to continually improve the

process of how you do something, at best you will keep getting the same good or great results instead of excellent results. Excellent performers are always looking for better ways to do things, and are not afraid of failure along the way until they achieve the more excellent result. Coaches are once again important in helping you make things better since they can see things you can't and give you the necessary perspective.

Why excellence?

So why is it so important to be an excellent performer instead of just a good or even great performer? It's important because there are a lot of good and great performers but only a handful of excellent performers. The excellent performers get noticed and have the greatest chance or opportunity to get ahead, who stand out in the crowd. I say *opportunity* to get ahead, because as difficult as excellent performance is to achieve, it only counts for about 10% of the PIE success formula. The I and the E count for the other 90% of getting ahead in the corporate world.

Without the first 10% of performance, however, the other 90% of I and E won't matter. Many would argue that excellent performance should account for more than 10%. That's how Harvey Coleman first presented it to me and what I have found to be true. While P only counts 10%, the smallest percentage among P, I, and E, it's probably the piece of PIE you will spend the most of your time on, perhaps as much as 50% to 75%.

Excellent performance is your entry or admission ticket into the corporate game as well as moving up the corporate ladder. Without it, you can't get past GO. P is how you build your reputation and build your legacy.

Excellent performance is the baseline for promotion and demonstrates you are ready and able to take on more responsibility. It's what gets and keeps you above the standard for the type of work you do.

An example

Let me close this section on performance with an example from my own career. The first position I had as a project manager was in 1977 when I was selected based on the planning and organization, decision-making, and communication skills I had demonstrated as an engineering manager. The project I was managing was the local New England implementation of an AT&T Bell System nationwide, automated accounting system, broken down into 35 to 40 sub-projects, with each sub-project headed by a district manager (one level above mine at the time).

There were two of us (managers) who also worked for a district manager responsible for overall coordination of the entire project. I was responsible for oversight of half of the sub-projects as was the other manager. To evolve into an excellent performer in this position, besides training and tutoring from my boss and the other manager, I also scheduled meetings with each sub-project team, not only mine but also those reporting to the other manager (I wanted to learn how all of the parts fit together). That gave me a good understanding of what each team was responsible for, the type of issues they were running into, who were the key people each sub-project team interacted with throughout the company and at AT&T, and also learned about the people running these sub-projects so I could more effectively interact with, guide, and support them (chemistry matters).

This process took three months and a lot of effort

on my part, but it was worth it. I become such an excellent performer at my job that when the other manager transferred, he was not replaced since I was deemed more than able to manage the entire project. Eighteen months later, I was promoted at AT&T to manage this project on a nationwide basis, recognized as the most effective project manager in the entire Bell System. This wasn't all I did to achieve excellent performance in this position, but I share this as one example of what it took then and takes now to achieve excellence. You only get out of something what you are willing to put into it.

Wherever you find yourself now on the corporate ladder, strive to achieve excellence at what you do, from cleaning the rest rooms to running an entire department to chairing the company board. It doesn't matter what you aspire to do because if you are not an excellent performer, chances are you will never get there. Become an excellent performer, and the possibility of realizing your career (and personal) dreams, goals, and aspirations will increase exponentially.

THE POWER OF
I AND E

Once you're an excellent performer, you still must address the I and E in the Power of PIE. I stated that those two letters account for 90% of your corporate success, so let's look at them more closely. By way of reminder the I and E stand for image and exposure, and work hand-in-hand. You can have the right image, but without exposure that image won't do you any good. Conversely, you can have exposure, but without the right image, the exposure won't be of much value to you. And of course, if you don't have excellent performance, image and exposure won't do much good either.

The Coleman PIE model attributes 30% of your corporate success to image and 60% to Exposure, but I've heard others maintain that it's 35% or 40% for image and 50% or 55% for exposure. The exact breakdown is not important, but based on my experience, exposure does matter more to your success than image. And while it requires a lot of effort to work on both, you will spend more time working on image than exposure.

I for image

Image is what other people think of you and your personal brand. It requires that you maintain a positive attitude and be someone who offers solutions and alternatives rather than just bringing up all the obstacles that a project or work initiative will face and have to overcome. Image is viewed by some as the message you send before you speak, and that includes attire, the confidence you exude, and your demeanor. It's something you want to develop early in your career, and says to those you interact with that you are ready for the corporate world (along with excellent performance). Every interaction you will ever have counts, so you want to do your best to project a positive image.

For me in terms of the *Power of PIE*, image means an appearance, representation, or likeness that reflects who I truly am. Others see that reflection through my "look and attitude" that is in line with what the company or corporation wants its customers and potential customers to see and be drawn to for business. It's part of the culture of the organization to which everyone is expected to conform. Those who don't conform and are not good performers will most likely not be with that company for long. Those who don't conform but are good, great, or excellent performers will be valued by the company for what they do, but most likely not progress very far up the corporate ladder as will be the case for those who do conform but are less than excellent performers. Those who do conform to the company image and are excellent performers, however, are the people who have the opportunity to move up the corporate ladder, *if* they get the right exposure.

When I started out in the corporate world in 1970, the "look" part of image was a lot easier to define and describe than today. In the '70s, for men the "look" was blue, black, or gray suits, white or light blue shirts with basic solid or striped ties, and black or brown laced shoes. For women, the dress code – suit and blouse/shirt and shoe colors – was the same, with skirts no shorter than down to just below the knee. Since women weren't seen as equals to men back then, most women didn't wear suit jackets and a pantsuit was a rarity.

Each decade since then, these rather strict expectations of image have changed as society has become more accepting of prevailing trends. In addition, during the '80s and '90s there were a myriad of training courses on dressing for success that corporations sponsored for their employees to attend. Even if we knew how the company wanted its high-potential employees to dress, it was a good idea to attend since it showed we were interested. Much less of this type of training is provided today because it's not seen as a prudent investment for companies. They expect people to pick this up on their own, which is a lot easier to do today than 30 or 40 years ago.

For white women as well as men and women of color, there are still other image hurdles that are much more difficult to overcome. People prefer to surround themselves with people similar to them in terms of gender, race, and age. While a little less stringent today than in the '70s, these "image" hurdles still exist in most if not every facet of society, including corporate America. On top of all the dress requirements, we had one or more strikes already against us if we were not a white male back then. That norm still exists since middle- to upper-class America is comprised mainly of white males, and people want others around them who look like they do.

On top of these hurdles, there were the additional image challenges for men and women of color, things like our speech (how we talk) and how we wore our hair. Imagine what it was like on June 21, 1970 when I reported to work for my first day wearing a mustard-colored suit, yellow shirt, and a yellow and black tie. I did not wear brown shoes but rather the high-heel boot variety popular with young black men at the time. Because of the Native American blood in me, my hair was not that much of a problem, as long as I kept it medium length and parted, and I had been well-trained to speak "white" when I had to. I also had a big flowing mustache and long sideburns.

Finally, men of color had one last hurdle women of any color didn't have, and that was our marital status. A single black man was considered a threat by white males to their white women. Yes, I said that. It was true then and it's true now. In fact, in the late '80s, a good friend of mine was about to be promoted and become the first black at the executive level of management in the company where I was employed at the time. He had recently divorced and was single, and was told point blank to his face that he really ought to consider getting married again, and the sooner the better! Rather than promote this well-qualified black man, the company waited a couple of years until another black male who conformed to their image of a black executive – he was married as well as qualified – was ready, and they promoted him.

I share all of this to make the point that when you hear talk about corporate image, it is more than just what is on the surface. If you are an excellent performer who has dreams and aspirations to move up in the corporate world, but don't have someone behind you who has your best interests at heart and will tell you the truth about what you need to do or not do to get ahead (fair or otherwise), you probably won't progress much beyond lower level positions in your company.

This is where mentors come in. They not only guide you on the external aspects of image, but also and most importantly, to the types of experiences you need to prepare for higher and higher positions with more and more responsibility, and what you have to do to get there. Mentors will guide you in terms of the type of exposure you need that will help you be recognized so you can impress those who can impact your career. A good mentor will also guide you to areas that another mentor may not be able to. I'll cover exposure in greater detail in the next section, but let me get back to image.

As is the case with striving to be an excellent performer, the choice is yours as to whether or not you want to do what needs to be done to conform as best you can (obviously, you cannot nor should you want to change the color of your skin) to the image that your company is looking for. Just as God will not make you receive Jesus as Savior or make you submit to Jesus as Lord, no one – not your company or your mentors or God for that matter – will force you to conform to the image your company is looking for. You must decide, and as you go through the decision-making process you need to educate yourself as to the consequences of your decision to conform or not conform. Either way, there are consequences. When you make the decision to conform or not, it's not an all-or-nothing decision.

You may opt to conform in certain areas but not in others, and that means you have a series of decisions to make. As you do, you need to consider whether or not conforming in an area compromises your values or belief system. If you are like me and have given your life to Christ, you must determine if conforming in any area is contrary to the word of God, or involves anything illegal, immoral, or ungodly. Remember, image is more than just external appearance, it also involves how you communicate, the stance or position you take on certain issues, your attitude, and more.

One contemporary example of the "more" we can look at regarding the issue of conforming or not conforming with the corporate image is what happened in the past regarding NFL quarterback Colin Kaepernick. Colin is a young man who was a rising star in the NFL, having taken his team to the 2013 Super Bowl. After that, his level of play slipped a little (translate that to mean he was no longer performing at an excellent level but still at a very good level), but he was better than some starting quarterbacks in the NFL and most of the back-up quarterbacks in the league.

After the 2016 season, he opted out of the last year of his contract with the San Francisco 49ers to test the free-agent market, which is commonplace for players in the last year of their contract. As I was writing this chapter at the start of the 2017 NFL season, Kaepernick still remained unsigned. Why is that, given he is as good or better than most of the starting or back-up quarterbacks in the NFL? In one word: image. Mr. Kaepernick decided to resist conformance with the unwritten image boundaries set by NFL owners.

Mr. Kaepernick used his position of visibility as

an NFL quarterback (exposure) to take a stand on the treatment of black people in America. He chose not just to speak out on the issue, as many athletes over the years have done like Jim Brown, Kareem Abdul-Jabbar, and Bill Russell, just to name a few. None of them were treated like Kaepernick, who as I write goes unsigned by any team in his sport. Several teams needed a good back-up quarterback and in some cases signed back-up quarterbacks not nearly as talented as Kaepernick. Why was this?

Kaepernick was not playing because he went beyond just speaking out on issues impacting blacks in America and found a creative way to draw attention to what he had to say. He sat on the bench and knelt on one knee during the playing of the National Anthem before the start of games during the 2016 NFL season. Many people thought this was un-American and not appropriate, but it did draw attention to the issues he felt were important.

Other players, black and white, supported what he did by kneeling with him or raising a clenched fist or locking arms during the playing of the National Anthem at pro, college, and high school levels. None of those players were unemployed as the 2017 football season progressed. Kaepernick also let his hair grow into a full-blown, sixties-era Afro to further draw attention to himself. He also backed up what he spoke out about by donating $1 million to various organizations that support black causes and a better quality of life for black people in America.

It is clear, despite the many denials from the NFL, that the reason he was not signed for the 2017 NFL season was because he chose to step out of the unwritten conformity contract that says players are required to stand during the playing of the National Anthem. That was the expected norm. Because Colin Kaepernick decided not to conform, he is not currently employed. Had his performance remained at the same excellent level it was in 2012, would he still be unemployed? I doubt it very much.

Because his performance slipped and even though he was still better than most quarterbacks in the NFL, the league used his performance as a reason for no team not signing him. The league also said some of its teams questioned his commitment to football because of his outspoken political views and active involvement outside football as he addressed the issues with which he is concerned. (They also raised concerns about his trip to Ghana in the summer of 2017 to try and find his ancestral roots.)

This book is not about Colin Kaepernick, but the point is that choosing not to conform to the image the NFL expects its players to project has cost him his job. It is a good example of how the impact of a person's decision to conform (or not) to their company's corporate image can impact how far that person can advance. Image matters in corporate America, and it matters in terms of the level of success one can achieve in a career. Don't get caught up in the thinking that if you work as hard as you can, you will get ahead. You may get rewarded for hard work or excellent performance, but without the right image, you most likely will not achieve your career goals.

Now let me share a personal example of the impact of image on one's career. It's an example of my decision not to conform to the corporate image, not because conforming was a bad decision but because it wasn't a God decision (dying to my own will and submitting to His will).

I had an opportunity in the mid-80s to take a position that would have allowed me to push through the glass ceiling and be promoted to what was referred to in my telecommunications company as a division manager, the fourth level of management. This would have put me on track to an executive management position within the next five years. It would have meant relocating back to the New York City area since that is where the position was. Working in New York was not the issue per se, but the main obstacle was uprooting my family again.

My wife was thrilled to be back in New England after I was transferred back to Boston from New York City, but then four years later we faced the possibility of moving again. All my wife's family and most of my family were in Massachusetts and Rhode Island. In addition, my son was in high school. We had to consider how he would perform at a new school and what kind of grades he would get with just two years before graduation and college looming on the horizon.

As a servant of God, I know the decisions I make, especially one as important as this one, should not be made without seeking God's wisdom on the matter, which I did. James 1:5-8 tells us that if we lack wisdom, we should ask God who will give it to us freely and without finding fault with us. The only requirement is that we ask in faith.

As I sought God in prayer, I was reminded of what my priorities should be as child of God. I'm not going to cover all those priorities here, but the first four priorities are what guided me in my decision. The top priority for all believers' lives is their personal relationship with God through Jesus Christ. The second is to take care of themselves physically, spiritually, and emotionally, because if they don't first take care of themselves, they won't be any good to help or care for anybody else. The third priority is their spouse if married or if not married, becoming the best single person they can be, with the fourth being their immediate family like children or other dependents.

With those priorities in mind, it didn't take me long to arrive at the correct, godly decision. It was not God's will for me to leave where I was at that time. He wanted me in New England, for what I wasn't sure, but I asked God for His wisdom in faith and was going with whatever He directed me to do because as a child of God, I must die to my will and live to do His. It was also clear to me that uprooting my wife and son at that time would not have been in our family's best interests. Part of me wanted to take the position so I could break through that glass ceiling on my corporate journey, but I also knew as a servant of God that my decisions weren't all about me, but for my family and others as well. Therefore, I turned down the promotion.

That was not what most people did back then. It was not the image of a high performer who wanted to get ahead. While most of my future assignments in telecommunications were challenging and paid well, because I "bucked" the system and did not fit the image that was expected by turning down that promotion to New York, I never got another promotion and never broke through the glass ceiling there. If I had it to do again, I would make the same decision. Why?

First and foremost, it was the God decision to make, the right decision to make for me. Beyond that, if I had gone back to New York, I may very well have not been led to the church I now attend in Providence, which the Lord clearly indicated is where He has wanted me to be for the past 18 years. Not being there could have resulted in forfeiting my growth in the Lord I have experienced there. I could possibly not have taken early retirement from the telecommunications industry when I did and then found my way to the healthcare industry where I had a productive second career and broke the glass ceiling, achieving an executive level of management, the first person of color in that company to do so. I very well would not have been close enough to care for my parents during their latter years when their health started to fail. The Word tells us in Ephesians 6 that we are to honor our mother and father so it will go well for us and have long life on earth. I still have a lot of growing to do in my walk with Christ, but that's one thing I got right – honoring my mother and father.

I could go on, but I hope you get the point. Let me close this section by stating that it is your choice whether you choose to be an excellent performer or not. It is your choice of whether you conform to the corporate image that is expected, and do all that is necessary to get the exposure you need with the right people to move your career ahead. Be sure to make the choice that is right for you, and is also a God choice as you yield to His will for your life over your own will. While I didn't take that promotion back in the late-1980s, looking back there is no question that in the long run things turned out much better for me, my family, and my career because I didn't take that promotion.

It's time to move on. Before I get into how the concepts of PIE interact and work with each other, let's talk about the E.

E FOR EXPOSURE

Exposure refers to who knows about you, and what you do and are capable of doing, both inside and outside of your organization. The word exposure itself has many definitions, but the best one in the context of the *Power of PIE* is *to present, view, exhibit, or display*. This is exemplified when a fashion model walks onto a runway wearing a designer's latest creations for all the world to see. If you are an excellent performer with the right image, then you need to present, exhibit, and display yourself to both potential mentors as well as others who can positively impact your career.

Mentors play a key role in helping you get the exposure you need with both other potential mentors and also those who can impact (have decision-making power over) your career. Networking is also a key tool in getting the exposure you need.

Your goal in getting that exposure with the right

people is to make sure they know who you are, what you've accomplished, and what you're capable of so you can leave an impression of "that's someone I'd like to have in my organization." Those with the power can help you in your career because of the potential they see in you. When you develop a plan (with a mentor) to get exposure with the right people, ask yourself: 1) what do I need to do to make sure they know who I am, what I've done and what I'm capable of? 2) how can I best interact with them? 3) have they seen me do any presentations? 4) have they seen anything that I've written? 5) what do others say to them about me? and 6) am I visible to them?

In general, people develop impressions about you based on what they see when they look at you, what they hear when you speak, what they take away from what and how you write, and what others say about you. Most executives and senior leaders are apt to be drawn to and want to build the next generation of leaders with people they have personal knowledge of and who are known by others who speak highly of them.

I can't tell you how many meetings, seminars, programs, social events, and so on I went to just to get exposure. I volunteered to work on many special projects and did other things my mentors thought I should do to get ahead and get the right exposure. Back in the late '70s when I was in my late twenties, I was a manager working for a district manager who was one of those rare people I told you about earlier – he was both a mentor and coach. His organization was responsible for overseeing implementation of a large project across the entire company, an assignment he inherited from his predecessor who, as it turned out, didn't have things running as smoothly as he was leading the executive team to believe. My boss was charged with trying to straighten things out.

I was his lead manager in the organization so the lead for this task fell on me. After several months of getting into the details of what was really going on and determining where things were not working very well in the implementation process, I came to my boss with a proposal that I thought within six months could turn the project around, get it back on track and completed within the original budget and schedule. After some back and forth with my boss and some fine tuning, the plan was ready to be presented to senior management. I developed the presentation, which my boss was to deliver on a Thursday afternoon.

Thursday morning my boss called me to inform me that he was ill, and I would have to make the presentation to his boss, the assistant vice president of the department as well as the vice president of the department who was the ultimate decision-maker for the proposal. My boss told me that he had already talked with his boss who I knew, and gave me some words of encouragement. He also started telling me about the vice president and the type of information he preferred about proposals like this one. When he mentioned the vice president's name, I almost fell out of the chair. This same vice president had been the vice president of the first department I worked in several years earlier. I'd only met him once, and he seemed like a tough, crusty, and difficult man to deal with.

My boss also told me several times that both his boss and the vice president were bottom-line people who liked to get right to the point. Armed with all this input, I tweaked the presentation a little bit and went off to the 2 PM meeting. You would think a proposal that would get the desired results and be completed on time and under budget would be a no-brainer to approve. This proposal, however, recommended we do some things differently than they had done before and could have been labeled radical. The proposal went into more detail than I might have wanted, but was easy to follow and understand, with sufficient back-up detail if needed. Like my pastor and others have said, if we want different or better results, we have to do something different. If the company wanted to get this project back on track, it would have to do some things differently (remember excellent performance?).

As soon as I walked in the door, the vice president yelled out "Russ Gross, how the hell are you?" Although I'd only met him once about six or seven years ago, he remembered me. (I don't know if it was because I was the first black manager he ever had in any of his organizations. I must have made a good impression.) The assistant vice president was shocked that his boss seemed to know me and remembered me so well. Keeping in mind what my boss told me, I started the presentation by giving them the bottom line, and said, "Now let me show you how we got there." Along the way, the assistant vice president tried to support me by interjecting some additional information, and finally the vice president said to him, "Shut up, George, the kid's doing okay on his own."

When I was done about 45 minutes later, the vice president said that was one of the best presentations he'd seen on such a complex project like the one I was working on. He added that the proposal made perfect sense, and he was going to recommend board approval. The project was approved and within six months was back on track and five months later came in on time, under budget, and with quality results.

How does this all relate to exposure? As it turns out, I learned from another mentor that my boss was not ill that day. He wanted me to have an opportunity to get the right exposure that would help me in my career. He later told me when I thanked him for the opportunity, he probably would not have done as good a job as I did for I knew the project far better than he did. It also doesn't hurt not to burn your bridges since you don't know when someone from your past can be just the person you need to support you for that next promotion. While that vice president never really became a mentor for me, it was because of his recommendation, along with that of the assistant vice president, that within the next seven months I was promoted to my first district manager position.

This is also a good example of how P, I, and E interact. Excellent performance led to a solution to a major obstacle, and my boss/coach/mentor (with the emphasis on mentor) helped me get the exposure I needed. Although I didn't know I would be presuming when I came to work that morning, I had been mentored in the "right" image to project, so I was dressed appropriately and not just for another day in the office. It was the *Power of PIE* in action!

Another thing I would do to get exposure was to volunteer to run the annual United Way campaign, which I mentioned briefly in an earlier chapter. Today that project has lessened in significance, but then it got me in front of a number of executives and senior managers who might not otherwise have been aware of who I was. Several of them were helpful to me in moving up the corporate ladder. In addition, with the help of several mentors and bosses, I got invited to higher-level, management strategy meetings on topics in which I was well versed. There executives and senior managers would not only meet and get to know me, but would also see what I had to contribute to the conversation toward a solution that could be successfully implemented. The most difficult thing about these meetings was to understand the protocol in the room and know when to speak or not. With coaching from mentors and bosses along the way, however, I was able to pick that up in a short period of time.

I said earlier that exposure is important both within and outside of the organization. This goes back to what I said in the chapter on mentors and how important it is to identify those people who can help you achieve both your career and personal goals. It's usually difficult to get an audience with people outside of your organization or company, so you must be more creative in what you do. This is where both networking and mentors really help. In my case, it was through contacts I already had by going to events and places where the people I wanted to be introduced to would be and then eventually actually meet with them. It usually takes several contacts and multiple events before you get to the person you really want to meet or be seen with. It's interesting that you usually meet other people along the way who can help you on your journey who you weren't even trying to get in front of.

One of the best things I ever did that got me a great deal of positive exposure was to get involved with what was categorized back in the '70s and '80s as an employee-affinity group. Those were organizations that worked with company management to enhance the training and development opportunities, network support groups, and advancement of underutilized employee groups such as women and minorities. In my case, it was the Minority Management Association (MMA) of New England Telephone Company, which after a couple of years of getting organized, was officially founded in 1979. The initial focus was on blacks (we hadn't got to the term African-American yet) and Hispanic employees.

Eventually, the focus expanded to Asian and other minority-group employees, with the name of the organization changing during the late '80s to the Multicultural Management Association, still preserving the MMA acronym while expanding to include union/non-management employees as well. As a result, the perception and position of minority employees improved over the years, especially from the mid-80s and beyond.

My MMA involvement, beyond being a charter member, was being on several working committees including a couple of committee chair positions, and eventually serving as vice president for two years and president for four years. I can't tell you how valuable most of the exposure was to my career, leading to a couple of key lateral moves and two promotions.

There was one experience, however, that involved all the components of PIE that was not that helpful in the short term, and where I had to decide if I was going to go with my Christian values and beliefs or the "corporate" thing to do. Obviously, my Christian values and beliefs won out, but my point is that I had to make a choice, realizing what the consequences of that decision might be. More specifically, during my second two-year term as MMA President, my job performance started to slip, not to the poor level, but it was no longer excellent, but mediocre or adequate. While there were factors beyond just me that played into this, I had to and did take full responsibility for my performance.

I got a call from the two most senior black executives in the company one day. Both were mentors of mine, who basically told me that it might be in my best interests to step down from the MMA presidency and focus more on my job performance as a signal to upper management that I did not put more value on the MMA work I was doing than my position at the company, which is what I was being paid for. I thanked them for their wise counsel, and said I needed time to think about it and would let them know my decision.

I understood their point and how I could have given the image that I was putting the MMA above my paying job. In addition, I suspected and eventually found to be true that they were asked to talk with me by at least one, maybe more, of my other non-black mentors who also were mentors to the two of them. Furthermore, I had already taken steps to get my performance back to the excellent level by seeking out coaches who could help me at the job level I was in at that time, even though I was a seasoned employee (we all need help periodically along our career and life journeys, no matter how far we may have already come).

I also knew I had to get my ego out of the way, which was telling me not to step down, so I turned to the Lord for His guidance. Once I did that, I stayed on and finished my term as MMA president. It was clear from my prayer time that the Lord had some additional work He wanted me to finish while I was MMA president, and that I should follow the path I had taken to improve my performance. As God always does, however, He had some other areas of my life He wanted to deal with where I was out of order, and which I had not thought were impacting my job performance – but they were.

The next three or four months were difficult, but as I have learned as a servant of God, we all must go through to get through – go through the darkness to get back to the light, go through a season of wilderness, and do this by faith in and submission to God's will for our lives over our own will. I did get through, my performance improved, and I finished the work I was to do while MMA president. But because I had "bucked" the system as it was, I didn't move along from where I was career-wise as quickly as I might have liked, but in the long term, the God decision was the right decision for me.

THE INTERSECTION OF PI AND E

I've shared the principles of PIE with you, and a little about the three key tools you need to effectively apply the PIE principles in your corporate (or life) journey: mentors, coaches, and networking. You may be asking where you get started? How do performance, image, and exposure interact with each other? Which comes first? Can you work on more than one at a time? In this chapter, I will answer those questions, sharing what I learned and what worked for me.

From my perspective, performance and the physical appearance part of image come first and can be worked on in conjunction with each other. Performance is your admission ticket to the game of moving up the corporate ladder, but you also want to make a good first impression when you walk in the door to not only your first assignment with a company, but also with each interaction you have and with each new assignment thereafter. I described my first day on the job earlier in this book, and if I had it to do all over again, I would have dressed more conservatively than I did, gotten a haircut, and trimmed my mustache. Before you go to any new assignment, do your homework and find out what is considered acceptable attire for the setting you will be working in.

Assuming you are dressing appropriately for the work environment you are in and have the right "look," most of your focus for the first several months will be on performance, learning to be the best you can possibly be at whatever your position is at the time. It's your work quality and ethic that will get you into the game and begin to catch people's attention and this is not just a one-time effort or something you work at whenever you move on to a new assignment.

Things change quickly in the world today, especially with the rapid pace of technological evolution, so you want to be sure you keep up with the latest methods and procedures, techniques, skills and technologies associated with the job you are in at any given time. That way you can stay at the top of your game and remain one of the best at what you do. Sometimes this may require you going above and beyond what you pick up or are able to learn on the job. You may need to take some outside courses or find coaches outside your company to learn what you need to remain an excellent performer, doing that on your own time and in some cases at your own cost.

All the while you are working at being an excellent performer and putting in more and more time at your company, stay alert for other aspects of the "corporate culture" that will be important to consider in establishing your brand/image in the company. This is the time when you start to identify potential mentors and network by getting involved in company activities that may not be directly related to your job but will help you with your image.

The goal is two-fold. One is to learn how things get done in your company, how people act and interact with each other, and how to behave in certain situations. This helps you gain a deeper understanding of the company's philosophy and values. Then you need to decide if you are willing to conform to these "corporate norms" in order to position yourself for the future. If you decide to conform, you want to find and work with mentors who can guide you in your career path, challenge you, and be brutally honest with you about what you will need to do or change to get ahead. If you don't want to conform, you still need to identify and work with mentors who can guide you in your career path in the same way.

Working with mentors also helps you prepare for the exposure aspect of PIE. Once you are an excellent performer, have established your brand, and are ready to get in front of those people who can help you in your career, those people may not yet know who you are. This is once again where mentors play a large role in getting you exposure, but you also have to be ready to create some of the exposure opportunities for yourself. If you're not willing to help yourself, why should a mentor want to help you?

And this is not a straightforward path from A to step B to step C. Performance, image, and exposure must continually interact with each other. I mentioned how you need to continue to work to keep up if you want to remain an excellent performer, and the same holds true for image and exposure. As society changes over time, so do corporate norms, which means you may have to adjust you image from time to time as well as your behavior, views, and what you support and don't support.

The same holds true for exposure. People leave companies to move on for a variety of reasons. When some of the people leaving are mentors, coaches, or other high-level executives who have had an influence on your career, you need to adjust to the new people, regardless of whether they are promoted from within or brought in from the outside. This may mean fine-tuning your brand or even moving to another position in the company as the opportunity presents itself, depending on what the new leadership thinks is important.

It definitely requires seeking opportunities for exposure with the new leadership at any level of the company that might impact you and your career, be it your direct supervisor, department head, or someone at the executive level. For example, you may be a first level manager in an organization when a new director is appointed for your department (assume two levels above you). You need to learn what that person values in terms of performance and image, which may require you tweaking how you do things and how you dress or act to continue to be an excellent performer projecting the right images, so you are still in a position to get the exposure you need to help further your career.

Having said all of this about how the elements of PIE interact and are iterative and not just a linear process, if pressed for a linear formula I would suggest the following:

1. Performance plus i (small i for appearance);

2. Image plus e (small e for initial exposure

opportunities to showcase your performance and brand so people who have the
ear of high-level decision-makers will talk
well of you);

3. Exposure

Again, P, I, and E are interactive and iterative, so the order above is meant to be guide and not a hard-and-fast rule.

Finally, as I have mentioned earlier in this book, during each step of the PIE process, you have decisions to make. Do you want to conform or not? Will conforming compromise your spiritual and personal values? What are the consequences of the decisions you make, in either direction, and can you live with them? As a believer, I seek God's wisdom and knowledge before making any major decision in my life, wanting to do His will for my life as opposed to my own will. I haven't always had a relationship with the Lord where that was important, and haven't always sought His wisdom and advice. What I have learned is that a God decision is always the best decision to make, even if it may not seem relevant to my present situation or circumstances. A God decision can change your situation or circumstances, so in time you will be victorious and successful!

EPILOGUE

An epilogue is defined as *a concluding part after the conclusion that summarizes the presentation just completed*. In this chapter, I will briefly summarize the principles and concepts that helped me be successful in my corporate career, which I've done my best to share in this book.

I'll start by saying that hard work does matter, but that alone will not get you ahead in the corporate world. It takes excellent performance, a personal brand or image that catches peoples' attention in a positive manner, and the opportunity to get in front of the right people who can both guide and influence your career and upward mobility in your chosen field.

These concepts are captured in the principles of PIE, which are performance, image, and exposure. Performance is your admission or entry ticket into the "corporate game" but only counts for about 10% of the success you will achieve (even though it is where you spend most of your time), with image and exposure counting for the other 90%. Three important tools you need to learn and master to successfully apply the power of PIE in your career are the use of coaches and mentors, along with the art of effective networking.

I've written this book not as the developer or father of the PIE principles. That distinction belongs to Mr. Harvey Coleman as I mentioned earlier, but I am a devoted advocate of the concept who took these principles and applied them, resulting in two successful careers. I've also tried to stress the importance of choices we all need to make with respect to our level of conformity to the standards of performance, image, and exposure wherever you are employed. The choices you make are personal and therefore will vary from one person to the next. What's important is that you understand the impact of each choice on your career, spiritual values, and personal values. Finally, while I've written this book from the perspective of succeeding in the corporate world, many if not all the principles, concepts, and tools discussed can be applied to your personal life as well.

My prayer is that the *Power of PIE* will be a blessing to you and important guidelines for both your corporate and personal journeys in life. Keep in mind, that sharing is caring, so if the *Power of PIE* is helpful to you, please share this book with others. If it's not that helpful to you, I ask that you still share it with others you know who may be helped in their corporate, professional, and/or personal lives by this book, so it can be a blessing to them.

Peace, and may the *Power of PIE* be with you.

Author's Note

If you are interested in learning more about PIE or networking, here are two sources I recommend that will give you added perspective and information.

3 Keys to Career Success: The Pieces of PIE, Mondo Frank, June 25, 2013 @mondofrank.com.

8 Networking Skills that Every Professional Needs to Have, Gregory Ciotti, @bidsketch.com.

To learn more about me or for a complete list of my products and services, go to:

www.faithprinciples.net

elderrussfaithprinciples@gmail.com

www.facebook.com/russellgross

@kings2acts
(Instagram)

@Rbgjr1Russ
(Twitter)